$\mathscr{S}$AVOURY
RICE DISHES

IMP Limited

CONTENTS

RICE FROM AROUND THE WORLD

There are over 8000 types of rice growing around the world. Here are the more common varieties you will find in your supermarket and some handy tips to get the best results.

HOW TO PREPARE RICE

• Most types of rice should be rinsed before cooking to remove any excess starch — this means the grains will stay separate and fluffy. There is no need to rinse or soak arborio or risotto rice.
• To rinse rice, put the grains into a large bowl and cover with cold water. Swirl the rice by hand, then tip out the cloudy water. Repeat three or four times until the water runs clear.

RICE TIPS

• For recipes where the rice grains should cling together, such as stuffings and risottos, use arborio, pudding or fragrant rice. If a recipe requires fluffy, separate grains of rice, such as a stir-fry or rice salad, always use long grain or basmati varieties.

• Rice absorbs flavours well. You may want to try cooking it with stock, fruit juice or milk instead of just water.
• For colourful rice, simply add saffron, turmeric or curry powder to the cooking liquid.
• To cool boiled rice quickly, put it into a large sieve set over a bowl. Prod the rice regularly with the handle of a clean wooden spoon to release the steam and heat.
• Once opened, keep packet rice in an airtight container in a cool, dry cupboard. Always check the best-before date on the packet.

EASY-COOK RICE

• Rice is not difficult to cook, especially if you follow the cooking instructions carefully (see p.62). As an alternative, most supermarkets stock easy-cook long grain rice. Pre-steamed before milling to seal in its nutrients, easy-cook rice is ideal for the novice as it ensures fluffy grains every time. Both white and brown types are available.

TYPES OF RICE

Long Grain Rice is mostly grown in the USA and India. The hulled and polished grains remain separate, firm and fluffy when cooked. Serve this rice as an accompaniment to spicy dishes such as Chilli con Carne.

Brown Rice has a nutty flavour and chewy texture and can be long, medium or short grain. As it is less refined than white, it needs longer cooking, although quick-cook varieties are also available.

Basmati Rice is grown in the foothills of the Himalayas. It is a fine, long grain rice with a delicate nutty flavour and is the best variety to eat with Indian food. Rinse the grains well before cooking to remove the excess starch.

Wild Rice is not a true rice, but the seeds of an aquatic grass which grows in Canada and the USA. It's expensive, but a little goes a long way as it absorbs four times its volume of water during cooking.

Fragrant Rice, also known as jasmine rice, is young, tender rice, popular in Thailand and Vietnam. Its delicate fragrance is often intensified by adding jasmine blossoms to the cooking water. It is usually served at special events, such as feast days.

Risotto Rice is a special short grain rice grown in northern Italy. The grains swell and cling together giving the dish its classic texture. Arborio is the best known of the risotto rices but others are available.

Short Grain Rice has small chalky grains which absorb a large amount of liquid and cook to a soft, sticky mass. It's mainly used for creamy desserts, milk puddings as well as savoury risottos.

Flaked Rice is white or brown rice that has been processed. It's quick to cook and mainly used for making puddings and fast porridges. The uncooked flakes can also be added to muesli mixtures.

GRENADIAN BAKED CHICKEN AND RICE

CARIBBEAN

Tender chicken pieces, marinated in aromatic spices, are slowly braised in the oven with sweet red peppers and fluffy rice to create this Caribbean island dish.

INGREDIENTS
(Serves 4)

- 500ml/18fl oz chicken stock
- 1 bay leaf
- 2 whole cloves
- 250g/9oz long grain rice
- 1kg/2¼lb chicken pieces
- salt and black pepper
- 3 tbsp groundnut oil, plus extra for greasing
- pinch of cayenne pepper
- pinch of ground nutmeg
- ½ tsp dried thyme
- 1 tbsp lemon juice
- 2 red peppers
- 1 red chilli
- 1 large onion
- 3 cloves garlic
- 40g/1½oz butter

INGREDIENTS TIP

Nutmeg has a pungent, sweet flavour and should be used sparingly. Alternatively, use a pinch of mixed spice.

1 Bring the stock to the boil in a saucepan with the bay leaf and cloves. Add the rice to the pan and simmer, uncovered, for 10 minutes. Remove from the heat and leave the rice to soak up the stock.

Step 1

2 Meanwhile, wash the chicken pieces, season and place in a shallow dish. Mix the oil, cayenne pepper, nutmeg, thyme and lemon juice. Brush over the chicken, cover and leave to marinate in the fridge for 1–2 hours.

Step 2

3 Preheat the oven to 180°C/350°F/Gas 4. Wash, halve and de-seed the red peppers. Cut into thick slices. Wearing rubber gloves wash, halve and de-seed the chilli, then slice finely. Peel and chop the onion and garlic.

4 Mix the peppers, chilli, onion and garlic with the rice and season with salt and pepper. Spoon the mixture into a greased shallow ovenproof dish or tin and arrange the chicken pieces in a single layer on top. Cut the butter into small pieces and dot over the chicken and rice. Bake for 40 minutes, or until the chicken is cooked through. If it starts to brown too much, cover with foil.

Step 4

Preparation **30** Min Marinating **1–2** Hours
Cooking **40** Min

Per Serving: 649 kcal/2728 kJ;
54g protein; 27g fat; 51g carbohydrate

TYPICALLY GRENADAN

The Caribbean island of Grenada, which is one of the small Windward islands, is famous for its high-quality spices. Nutmeg is exported worldwide and is used to flavour a variety of dishes, especially milk- and egg-based recipes such as custards, béchamel and bread sauces.

COOKING TIPS

If you want the chicken to be very crisp, brown the marinated pieces in 3 tablespoons oil before placing them in the oven • The dish can also be cooked in a special clay chicken brick, but remove the lid halfway through cooking or the condensation from the lid will stop the chicken cooking properly.

SERVING TIP

Sprinkle the chicken with toasted flaked coconut and accompany with a spicy chilli sauce and lemon wedges.

 Serve with freshly squeezed orange juice with a dash of grenadine syrup.

SERVING TIP Serve with toasted coconut flakes and a crunchy mixed salad.

 Planter's Punch makes a refreshing aperitif. Mix together white rum, lemon juice and orange juice.

CARIBBEAN RICE WITH FISH

CARIBBEAN

French finesse with a touch of the exotic typifies the cuisine of many West Indian islands. Here, the rice retains the delicate aroma of bay leaves, while the fish is scented with allspice.

INGREDIENTS
(Serves 4)

- 7 allspice berries
- 575g/1¼lb cod fillet
- salt and black pepper
- juice of 2 limes
- 500ml/18fl oz chicken stock
- 2 bay leaves
- 200g/7oz long grain rice
- 500g/1lb 2oz tomatoes
- bunch of spring onions
- 3 tbsp groundnut oil
- 2 tbsp white rum

TO GARNISH

- 1 lime
- 50g/2oz pimiento-stuffed green olives

INGREDIENTS TIP

Cod is the perfect fish for this recipe as its firm, white flesh flakes easily when cooked. Haddock makes a tasty alternative.

1 Finely crush 4 allspice berries using a pestle and mortar. Cut the cod into bite-sized pieces and season. Squeeze the juice from the limes and stir in the crushed allspice. Put the cod on a plate and pour over the lime juice mixture.

2 Put the stock, bay leaves, remaining whole allspice berries and a pinch of salt into a saucepan and bring to the boil. Add the rice, cover and simmer for 15 minutes.

3 Put the tomatoes in a bowl and cover with boiling water. Leave for 30 seconds, drain, then cut a slit in the skin. Peel, de-seed and dice the tomatoes. Trim and slice 3 of the spring onions. Add the tomatoes and onions to the rice and cook for 5 minutes.

4 Remove the fish from the marinade and pat dry with kitchen paper; reserve the marinade. Heat the oil in a pan and fry the fish for about 5 minutes, turning once.

5 Add the lime marinade and rum to the pan. Simmer for 2 minutes until the fish is cooked. Spoon rice onto a plate and place the fish on top. Garnish with the remaining spring onions, lime slices and olives.

Step 1

Step 3

Step 5

Preparation **25** Min Cooking **15** Min
Per Serving: 430 kcal/1800 kJ;
32g protein; 25g fat; 52g carbohydrate

TYPICALLY CARIBBEAN

Allspice is one of the Caribbean's most widely grown spices, and the French West Indian island of Martinique exports a large part of its crop. Also known as pimento, allspice combines the flavours of cloves, cinnamon and nutmeg.

ℳEXICAN RICE AND BEEF BAKE

MEXICO

INGREDIENTS
(Serves 4)

- 1 onion
- 2 cloves garlic
- 3 celery sticks
- 1 tbsp sunflower oil, plus extra for greasing
- 1 tsp dried oregano
- ¼ tsp ground cloves
- 400g/14oz minced beef
- 1 tsp plain flour
- salt and black pepper
- pinch of cayenne pepper
- 250ml/9fl oz passata
- 125ml/4fl oz beef stock
- 200g/7oz long grain rice
- 250g/9oz mozzarella
- 50g/2oz Emmental cheese
- 50g/2oz sunflower seeds
- flat-leaved parsley, to garnish

INGREDIENTS TIP
Jars and cartons of sieved tomatoes, called passata, can be bought in supermarkets. Any thick tomato pasta sauce could also be used.

This Mexican speciality of rice and minced beef flavoured with oregano and cloves is very popular in the south of the country. Melted cheeses and sunflower seeds make a delicious topping.

1 Peel and finely chop the onion and garlic. Wash and chop the celery. Heat the oil in a saucepan, then add the onion and garlic. Stir in the oregano and cloves.

Step 1

2 Add the mince to the pan and fry it for 5 minutes until browned, stirring occasionally. Add the flour and the chopped celery, then season with salt, pepper and cayenne pepper. Add the tomato passata and pour in the stock. Stir, bring to the boil, then cover and simmer for 25 minutes.

Step 2

3 Meanwhile, cook the rice in lightly salted, boiling water for 20 minutes, then drain. Preheat the oven to 180°C/350°F/Gas 4. Mix the rice with the meat mixture and transfer it all to a greased ovenproof dish.

4 Cut the mozzarella into thin slices and place evenly over the rice. Grate Emmental over the top. Bake for 30 minutes, or until the cheese is crispy. If the topping browns before the end of cooking time, cover with foil.

Step 5

5 Dry-fry the sunflower seeds in a frying pan over a medium heat for 3 minutes until lightly browned. Sprinkle on top of the cheesy topping. Garnish with parsley.

Preparation **45** Min Cooking **30** Min
Per Serving: 741 kcal/3099 kJ;
37g protein; 45g fat; 51g carbohydrate

TYPICALLY MEXICAN
The town of Oaxaca in southern Mexico is renowned for its meat and poultry recipes which incorporate bitter chocolate. Queso de Oaxacai, a locally produced Cheddar-type cheese has a slightly sour taste and would be used in savoury bakes like this one.

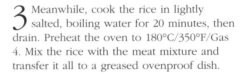

COOKING TIP

Select lean minced beef which contains very little fat, or ask your butcher to grind a lean cut for you, since more economical cuts can produce a lot of fat when fried. To avoid an over-greasy finished dish, spoon off all but 1 tablespoon of fat from the pan before adding the tomato passata and stock in step 2.

SERVING TIP

For those who love the hot tastes of Mexico, serve with pickled chillies and slices of cucumber and tomato.

 Try a refreshing drink of cranberry juice diluted with sparkling mineral water.

$\mathcal{A}$CAPULCO PEPPERS

MEXICO

This hot, spicy risotto with tomatoes and peppers is one of Mexico's favourite dishes. Its colours are those of the national flag — green, white and red.

INGREDIENTS
(Serves 4)

- 500g/1lb 2oz tomatoes
- 1 spring onion
- 2 tbsp chopped fresh parsley or 1 tsp dried
- 2 pickled Jalapeño chillies or large fresh chillies
- salt and black pepper
- 1 small onion
- 2 cloves garlic
- 2 green peppers
- 2 fresh corn-on-the-cob or 400g/14oz can sweetcorn
- 2 tbsp sunflower oil
- 250g/9oz long grain rice
- ¼ tsp ground cumin
- 500ml/18fl oz chicken stock

INGREDIENTS TIP
Jalapeños are large, dark green chillies. They are very hot so if you prefer a milder taste, de-seed the chillies before adding them to the tomatoes.

1 Place the tomatoes in a bowl and pour over boiling water to cover. Leave for 1 minute, then drain and peel off the skin. Remove the seeds and dice the flesh. Trim the spring onion and chop coarsely. Mix together tomatoes, spring onion and parsley.

Step 2

2 Wearing rubber gloves, wash the Jalapeño chillies and cut into thin rings. Stir into the tomato mixture, then season with salt and pepper.

3 Peel and chop the onion and garlic. Wash, halve and de-seed the green peppers, then slice thinly. If using corn-on-the-cob, boil for 10 minutes in water. Drain and cool, then remove the kernels from the cob with your fingers or a knife. Or, if using canned sweetcorn, drain away the liquid.

Step 3

4 Heat the oil in a frying pan and cook the onion and garlic until transparent. Add the peppers, rice and sweetcorn kernels and cook for 2–3 minutes. Season with salt, pepper and cumin and add the stock and tomato mixture. Simmer for 15 minutes, or until the rice is cooked (see Cooking Tip), stirring occasionally. Serve hot.

Step 4

Preparation **35** Min Cooking **15** Min
Per Serving: 439 kcal/1860 kJ;
8g protein; 11g fat; 82g carbohydrate

TYPICALLY ACAPULCO
Long before Acapulco became a mecca for tourists, it was the busiest Pacific coast trading port between Mexico and the Orient. Spanish merchants arrived in cargo ships laden with precious silks and spices, such as cumin from Asia.

COOKING TIP

Cooking times for long grain rice can vary according
to the brand you buy, so you may need to simmer
the mixture for slightly less time or a little longer
than the 15 minutes recommended in step 4. You may
also need to add a little extra stock or water if the
rice absorbs all the liquid before it is fully cooked.

SERVING TIP

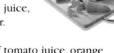

Garnish with finely sliced pieces of
avocado, tossed in lemon or lime juice,
and sprinkle with fresh coriander.

Sangrita — a Mexican mix of tomato juice, orange
juice and lime juice makes an ideal cooler.

CALIFORNIAN RICE PANCAKES

USA

The Californians enjoy cooking with their wine as well as drinking it. Here, vegetables slowly simmered in white wine are served with golden pancakes made from rice.

INGREDIENTS
(Serves 4)

- 3 large eggs
- 175ml/6fl oz milk
- 125g/4½oz plain flour
- salt and white pepper
- 250g/9oz long grain rice
- 2 small courgettes
- 2 tomatoes
- 1 yellow pepper
- 5 tbsp sunflower oil
- 100ml/3½fl oz white wine
- 100ml/3½fl oz vegetable stock
- 75g/3oz tomato purée
- 1 tbsp sunflower seeds
- 25g/1oz Parmesan cheese
- 1 tbsp chopped fresh basil

INGREDIENTS TIP

Sunflower seeds add a crunchy, nutty texture to the dish and are available from most supermarkets.

1 Beat the eggs, milk, flour, salt and pepper together to make a smooth batter. Leave to stand while you cook the rice. Boil the rice according to the packet instructions. Drain, then cool by running cold water through the rice. Drain again and add to the batter.

Step 1

2 Wash the courgettes and cut into thin sticks. Cover the tomatoes with boiling water, leave for 1 minute, then drain and peel the skin with a knife. De-seed and slice. Halve the pepper, de-seed and dice.

Step 2

3 Preheat the oven to 130°C/250°F/Gas ½. Heat 2 tablespoons of oil in a saucepan and gently brown the courgettes and pepper. Add the tomatoes and season. Stir in the wine, stock and tomato purée. Simmer over a low heat for 10 minutes.

4 Meanwhile, heat the remaining oil in a frying pan. Spoon about 2 tablespoons of batter into the pan for each pancake. Fry in batches for 2–3 minutes, turning once. Remove when golden and keep warm in the oven. Dry-fry the sunflower seeds in a frying pan for 30 seconds. Serve the pancakes with the sauce and sunflower seeds. Grate the Parmesan and sprinkle on top with the basil.

Step 4

Preparation **35** Min Cooking **20** Min

Per Serving: 596 kcal/2498 kJ; 17g protein; 29g fat; 68g carbohydrate

TYPICALLY CALIFORNIAN

California's sunny climate is ideal for growing grapes. New World wines, which use Chardonnay and Zinfandel grapes produced in the Napa and Sonoma valleys, are among the finest in the world. Californian grapes are also dried to make plump, juicy raisins.

COOKING TIP

Any other rice can be used in these pancakes. You may need to allow longer preparation time as the cooking time for rice varies according to type. Brown rice, for example, which has a coarser texture and nuttier flavour, takes 15-20 minutes longer to cook than long grain white rice.

SERVING TIP

For a light supper, serve the pancakes with a mixed green salad tossed in vinaigrette dressing.

🍷 Try a refreshing spritzer of white wine with a dash of orange juice, topped up with mineral water.

SERVING TIP Serve this Jambalaya with whole-grain mustard to complement the sausage and ham.

 Try lager or light beer on its own, or mixed with lemonade to make a shandy.

JAMBALAYA

USA

This famous Creole rice dish is typical of the spicy cooking of America's Deep South. Golden morsels of fried turkey, ham and sausage are coated in a red-hot seasoning.

INGREDIENTS
(Serves 4)

- 400g/14oz turkey breast
- 100g/4oz smoked ham
- salt and black pepper
- ¼ tsp cayenne pepper
- 3 sticks celery
- 1 green pepper
- 2 onions
- 2 cloves garlic
- 125g/4½oz smoked pork sausage
- 250g/9oz long grain rice
- 2 tbsp sunflower oil
- 125ml/4fl oz chicken stock
- 200ml/7fl oz tomato passata
- pinch of cinnamon

INGREDIENTS TIP

The traditional recipe for Jambalaya uses heavily seasoned tasso smoked ham. You can substitute any smoked ham and season with cayenne and black pepper.

1 Cut the turkey into bite-sized pieces. Cut the ham into thick slices and then into 5cm/2in strips. Season both with black pepper and a sprinkling of cayenne pepper. Season the turkey with salt.

2 Wash, trim and slice the celery. Halve the pepper, de-seed and slice thinly. Peel and chop the onions and garlic. Remove the skin from the smoked sausage and cut into thick slices with a sharp knife.

3 Cook the rice in a saucepan of lightly salted, boiling water for about 20 minutes or until the grains are tender.

4 Meanwhile, heat the oil in a saucepan and stir-fry the turkey and ham for 5 minutes. Add the onion, garlic, celery, pepper and sausage slices and fry gently for 2 minutes. Add the chicken stock and passata, then season with salt, pepper and cinnamon. Cover and simmer over a gentle heat for about 10 minutes until the vegetables are tender. Adjust the seasoning if necessary.

5 When the rice is cooked, drain and spoon onto a warmed serving dish. Top with the meat and vegetables.

Step 2

Step 4

Step 4

Preparation **30** Min Cooking **20** Min
Per Serving: 541 kcal/2274 kJ;
37g protein; 23g fat; 48g carbohydrate

TYPICALLY LOUISIANA

Chefs in New Orleans, in Louisiana, claim that their dishes wake up every taste bud. Cayenne pepper or chillies are added to many dishes, such as Gumbo (a meat and vegetable stew). Local specialities can be sampled each year at the city's colourful Mardi Gras festival.

WILD RICE WITH SALMON

USA

INGREDIENTS
(Serves 4)

- 200g/7oz mixed wild and long grain rice
- salt and black pepper
- 1 onion
- 1 large fennel bulb
- 1 tbsp sunflower oil
- 90ml/3fl oz dry white wine
- 90ml/3fl oz double cream
- 500g/1lb 2oz salmon fillet, skinned
- 2 tbsp lemon juice
- 1 bunch fresh dill

INGREDIENTS TIP

You can buy packets of mixed wild and long grain rice at most supermarkets. If you want to mix it yourself, use 50g/2oz wild rice and 150g/5oz long grain rice. However, as wild rice is expensive, it may be cheaper to buy it ready-mixed.

A mixture of wild and long grain rice is the perfect base for generous chunks of salmon cooked with fennel and onions in a delicious cream and wine sauce.

1 Place the rice in a sieve and rinse by briefly running cold water through it. Bring a pan of lightly salted water to the boil and simmer the rice for about 25 minutes, or until tender. Drain and keep warm.

2 Meanwhile, chop the onion. Trim and wash the fennel. Halve and slice finely. Heat the oil in a saucepan, add the onion and cook for 3 minutes until transparent.

3 Add the fennel and cook for 2 minutes, stirring occasionally. Season with salt and pepper, pour in the wine and cream and cook for a further 3–4 minutes.

4 Cut the salmon into 3cm/1½in cubes. Season with salt and pepper and sprinkle with the lemon juice. Add to the pan, cover, and cook gently for 5 minutes, until the salmon is opaque.

5 Wash the dill and shake it dry. Reserve four sprigs and finely chop the remainder. Stir into the cooked rice. Divide the rice between four plates, spoon the salmon and vegetables on top and garnish with the dill sprigs. Serve immediately.

Step 1

Step 4

Step 5

Preparation **30** Min Cooking **25** Min
Per Serving: 610 kcal/2550 kJ;
30g protein; 34g fat; 45g carbohydrate

TYPICALLY MINNESOTAN
Wild rice is not rice at all, but the seed of an aquatic grass. It grows by the lakes and rivers of the northern state of Minnesota. Originally, native Americans harvested the rice from small boats and it is therefore sometimes known as Indian rice.

COOKING TIP

It is important never to overcook fish as the delicate flesh quickly dries out and loses flavour and texture. After adding the salmon chunks to the pan, keep the heat very low and cook only until the flesh turns evenly pale and opaque. Serve immediately so that the salmon doesn't continue to cook.

SERVING TIP

Serve with a platter of hard-boiled eggs topped with red caviar and garnished with fresh dill.

 A golden Californian Chardonnay is delicious served with this light fish dish.

3 WAYS WITH RICE SALAD

Rice salads are ideal for parties and picnics. It's so easy to adapt one basic recipe to suit all occasions by adding fish, cold meats or cheese.

BASIC RICE SALAD RECIPE

Preparation **15** Min   Cooking **12** Min   Standing **1** Hour

(SERVES 4)
- salt and black pepper
- 150g/5oz long grain rice

FOR THE DRESSING
- 5 tbsp white wine vinegar
- 5 tbsp sunflower oil
- 2 tbsp fresh chives
- 2 shallots

1 Bring a pan of salted water to the boil and simmer the rice for 12 minutes, or until cooked but still chewy. Drain and leave to cool.

2 Prepare the dressing by whisking the vinegar, oil, salt and pepper together in a small bowl.

3 Wash and chop the chives. Peel and chop the shallots. Add to the dressing and stir in with a metal spoon.

4 Reserve half the dressing. Stir the rest into the rice, then leave the rice to stand for 1 hour, for the flavours to develop.

THREE FISH MEDLEY

Preparation **20** Min

NORWAY
- 2 tbsp fresh dill or 1 tsp dried
- 2 tbsp sour cream
- 1 tsp creamed horseradish
- 200g/7oz smoked salmon
- 100g/4oz smoked trout fillet
- 1 smoked mackerel fillet
- salt
- 1 lemon
- 1 hard-boiled egg

5 Follow steps 1–4 from the basic recipe. Mix the dill, sour cream and horseradish with the prepared dressing. Cut all the fish into small pieces and mix with the sour cream mixture.

6 Add the rice to this mixture and season. Garnish with the lemon and egg, cut into wedges.

CHEESE AND NUT SALAD

Preparation **30** Min

SWITZERLAND

- 150g/5oz Emmental
- 50g/2oz Parma ham
- 200g/7oz black grapes
- 1 red apple
- juice of ½ lemon
- 8 cherry tomatoes
- 3 tbsp crème fraîche
- 50g/2oz walnuts, chopped

5 Follow steps 1–4 from the basic rice recipe. Cut the cheese into sticks and cut the ham into thin slices. Mix the ham and the cheese with the rice.

6 Wash the grapes and pat dry. Halve and remove the seeds.

7 Wash the apple, core and slice into bite-sized pieces, then sprinkle with lemon juice to prevent them discolouring.

8 Wash the tomatoes and slice in half. Add the grapes, apple and tomatoes to the rice. Mix the crème fraîche with the reserved dressing from the basic recipe, and stir into the salad. Sprinkle the walnuts on top.

SALAMI AND PEPPER SALAD

Preparation **25** Min

HUNGARY

- 100g/4oz salami, sliced
- 1 red pepper
- 198g/7oz can sweetcorn
- ½ tsp ground paprika
- 1 tsp Dijon mustard
- 150ml/¼ pint sour cream
- chopped fresh parsley or chives

5 Follow steps 1–4 of the basic rice salad recipe.

6 Cut the salami into 1cm/½in pieces. Wash the pepper, halve, de-seed and slice thinly. Drain the sweetcorn.

7 Mix the prepared dressing from the basic recipe with the paprika, mustard and sour cream.

8 Mix the salami, sliced pepper and sweetcorn into the rice, with the creamy dressing, then stir in the parsley or chives.

CHICKEN FRIED RICE

CHINA

Bite-sized slices of chicken are glazed in soy sauce and sherry before stir-frying with crisp, sliced vegetables and fluffy rice for a quick, all-in-one meal.

INGREDIENTS
(Serves 4)

- salt
- 250g/9oz long grain rice
- 400g/14oz chicken breasts, skinned
- 3 tbsp soy sauce
- 1 tbsp dry sherry
- ½ tsp caster sugar
- 1 tsp cornflour
- 1 red pepper
- bunch of spring onions
- 3 leaves of Chinese leaf
- 2cm/¾in piece root ginger
- 2 cloves garlic
- 4 tbsp sunflower oil
- 1 tbsp chopped fresh chervil plus extra sprigs, to garnish

INGREDIENTS TIP

Soy sauce is made from soya beans and is available in light or dark styles, dark having the more concentrated and intense flavour. You can use either sort in this recipe.

1 Bring a pan of lightly salted water to the boil. Add the rice and cook for about 12 minutes, or until the grains are tender. Drain in a colander.

2 Slice the chicken breasts. In a large bowl mix together the soy sauce, sherry, sugar and cornflour. Add the chicken, toss to coat, and marinate for 15 minutes.

Step 2

3 Wash the pepper and spring onions. Cut the pepper in half, remove the seeds and slice. Chop the spring onions, wash the Chinese leaf and shred. Peel the ginger and garlic and chop finely.

Step 3

4 Heat the oil in a wok or large frying pan. Briefly stir-fry the garlic and ginger, ensuring they don't burn. Add the chicken mixture and stir-fry for 1 minute over a brisk heat until golden brown, turning constantly.

5 Add the vegetables and stir-fry for about 30 seconds. Add the rice and toss all the ingredients together. Stir-fry for about 2 minutes until heated through. Sprinkle with the chervil and serve immediately in four bowls, garnished with a chervil sprig.

Step 5

Preparation **15** Min Marinating **15** Min
Cooking **20** Min
Per Serving: 430 kcal/1803 kJ;
26g protein; 20g fat; 39g carbohydrate

TYPICALLY CANTONESE

Stir-frying is the most popular style of cooking in Hong Kong and the southern Chinese city of Canton. Meat, fish and vegetables are cut into bite-sized pieces, added gradually to a very hot wok and stirred constantly so they cook evenly and quickly.

COOKING TIP

The rice can be cooked 2–3 hours in advance and the chicken prepared and left to marinate for a similar length of time. Prepare everything before you start cooking as stir-frying is a rapid process, and the ingredients should be added to the pan in quick succession. Serve immediately everything is cooked.

SERVING TIP

Have a small bowl of soy sauce on the table so that everyone can add more if they wish.

 A cup of Chinese green or jasmine tea is refreshing served with this dish.

$\mathscr{S}$PECIAL MALAYSIAN RICE

MALAYSIA

Ribbons of stir-fried vegetables are drizzled with aromatic sesame oil and tossed with a delicious mix of succulent prawns, crisp beansprouts and fried rice.

INGREDIENTS
(Serves 4)

- salt and black pepper
- 250g/9oz long grain rice
- 1 onion
- 3 garlic cloves
- 3 spring onions
- 1 carrot
- 150g/5oz beansprouts
- 3 tbsp sunflower oil
- 2 tsp sesame oil
- 275g/10 oz peeled prawns
- pinch of cayenne pepper
- 2 tbsp chopped fresh parsley

INGREDIENTS TIP

Cayenne pepper is a fiery spice ground from the flesh and seeds of dried chilli peppers. Add sparingly, so that its heat does not overpower other ingredients.

1 Bring a pan of lightly salted water to the boil. Add the rice and cook according to the packet instructions. Peel and chop the onion and garlic. Trim, wash and chop the spring onions and peel and slice the carrot. Place the beansprouts in a sieve and rinse under cold running water for about 30 seconds. Leave to drain.

Step 1

2 Heat 2 tablespoons of sunflower oil in a frying pan, add the onion and garlic and stir-fry over a high heat for 1 minute.

3 Add the carrot and spring onions and fry for a further 2 minutes. Transfer all the vegetables from the pan to a large bowl. Season to taste and add the sesame oil.

Step 3

4 Heat the remaining sunflower oil in the frying pan, add the prawns and stir-fry for 2 minutes. Season with salt, pepper and cayenne. Stir in the rice and beansprouts and stir-fry for a further 2 minutes.

5 Return the vegetables to the pan and toss together for about 3 minutes until heated through. Sprinkle with the chopped parsley and serve.

Step 4

Preparation **15** Min Cooking **20** Min
Per Serving: 377 kcal/1585 kJ;
20g protein; 14g fat; 45g carbohydrate

TYPICALLY MALAYSIAN

A large Chinese community has been living and trading in Malaysia for thousands of years. Along with the myriad of dishes they brought with them, the Chinese also introduced the cooking technique of stir-frying — now an integral part of Malaysian cuisine.

COOKING TIP

Either cooked or raw peeled prawns can be used for this dish. If frozen, both sorts need thorough defrosting before cooking. Cooked prawns just need tossing over the heat for a couple of minutes to heat them through. Raw prawns need to be cooked until they turn from grey-green to pink — about 3-4 minutes.

SERVING TIP

Serve the Malaysian rice with spicy condiments such as a fiery, red chilli paste and soy sauce.

 Slightly sweetened iced tea with a squeeze of lemon juice goes well with this dish.

SERVING TIP Serve with a salad of sliced spring onions and celery, sprinkled with chopped fresh herbs.

 A light, chilled beer or glass of sparkling mineral water makes a refreshing accompaniment.

COCONUT AND VEGETABLE RICE

MALAYSIA

Simmering in fragrant coconut milk flavours the mange tout, carrots and spring onions in this tempting Malaysian treat. Serve with rice, and top with finely sliced, fiery chillies.

INGREDIENTS

(Serves 4)

- 150g/5oz mange tout
- 4 spring onions
- 250g/9oz carrots
- 1 lime
- salt and black pepper
- 275g/10oz Thai jasmine fragrant rice or long grain rice
- 100g/4oz coconut milk powder
- 2 tbsp sunflower oil
- 2 red chillies
- 1 bunch coriander or flat-leaved parsley
- bunch of chives
- 3 tbsp fish sauce or soy sauce

INGREDIENTS TIP

You can use 425ml/14fl oz canned coconut milk in place of the coconut powder. Coconut powder is available from large supermarkets or oriental stores.

1 Top and tail the mange tout and wash and slice the spring onions. Peel and thinly slice the carrots.

2 Wash the lime and pat dry. Remove the peel with a sharp knife and cut into fine shreds. Squeeze the juice from the lime into a small bowl. Bring a pan of lightly salted water to the boil, cook the rice for about 12 minutes, or until tender, then drain. Place in a serving dish and keep warm.

3 Whisk the coconut powder into water following packet instructions. Heat the oil in a saucepan and stir-fry half the spring onions, the mange tout and carrots for 2–3 minutes. Season with salt and pepper. Add the coconut milk and half the lime peel. Simmer for 10 minutes, stirring occasionally.

4 Wearing rubber gloves, slice the chillies lengthways, de-seed and chop finely. Chop the coriander or parsley, and the chives. Spoon the vegetables over the rice and sprinkle over the remaining lime peel and chillies. Mix the fish sauce or soy with the lime juice, serve separately. Accompany with the coriander and remaining spring onions.

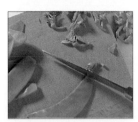

Step 1

Step 2

Step 3

Preparation **25** Min Cooking **20** Min
Per Serving: 364 kcal/1532 kJ;
7g protein; 14g fat; 57g carbohydrate

TYPICALLY MALAYSIAN

Black peppercorns are the berries of the Piper nigrum plant, which grows all over south-east Asia. The berries are picked while green, then dried in the sun to shrivel and darken them. Ground black pepper is the world's most popular spice.

INDONESIAN RICE WITH BEANSPROUTS

INDONESIA

INGREDIENTS
(Serves 4)

- 8 chillies
- 250g/9oz long grain rice
- 100g/4oz frozen peas
- 150g/5oz boneless cooked chicken
- 4cm/1½in piece root ginger
- 1 clove garlic
- 1 onion
- 3 tbsp groundnut oil
- 150g/5oz peeled shrimps
- salt and black pepper
- 100g/4oz beansprouts
- 6 tbsp chicken stock
- 1 tsp sambal oelek paste
- ½ tsp ground turmeric
- 1 egg
- 1 tbsp milk

INGREDIENTS TIP

Sambal oelek is a fiery, red, chilli paste available from Asian shops or large supermarkets. Any chilli sauce can be used in this recipe.

Well known in the Far East as Nasi Goreng, this Indonesian meal is a delicious mix of shrimps, golden nuggets of chicken and fried rice flavoured with stock and chilli.

1 Prepare the chilli flower garnish. First, make cuts close together from the point of each chilli almost to the stalk. Leave in a bowl of iced water for 2–3 hours until they curl.

2 Cook the rice according to the packet instructions, then drain. Cook the peas in a separate pan of boiling water for 5 minutes, then drain. Cut the chicken into bite-sized pieces. Peel and grate the ginger and peel and finely slice the garlic and onion.

3 Heat 2 tablespoons of oil in a large frying pan or wok. Add the ginger, garlic and onion and stir-fry for 5 minutes. Add the chicken and shrimps and stir-fry for a further 4 minutes. Season.

4 Rinse the beansprouts. Stir the stock and rice into the chicken and shrimps. Add the sambal oelek, then the peas, beansprouts and turmeric. Stir-fry for 2 minutes.

5 Beat the egg and milk together. Heat the remaining oil in a frying pan, pour in the egg mixture and fry briefly on both sides to make a thin omelette. Remove from the pan, cut into thin strips and scatter over the rice mixture. Garnish with the chilli flowers.

Step 2

Step 3

Step 4

Chilling **2–3** Hours Preparation **40** Min
Cooking **35** Min
Per Serving: 437 kcal/1838 kJ;
24g protein; 18g fat; 46g carbohydrate

TYPICALLY INDONESIAN
Nasi Goreng and Bami Goreng are popular Indonesian dishes. The combination of cooked meats, seafood, spices and vegetables topped with shredded omelette is the same for both dishes but Nasi Goreng is made with rice and Bami Goreng with rice noodles.

COOKING TIP
When frying garlic, it is important not to let it burn. As the cloves contain a lot of oil, they tend to brown quickly, but if cooked too quickly on a high heat they develop a bitter flavour. If frying garlic with onions, keep the heat low so both the garlic and onions soften and their flavours become mellow and sweet.

SERVING TIP
Serve on cucumber slices instead of the traditional banana leaf. Try a poached egg instead of the omelette.

Serve freshly squeezed orange juice or another fruit juice, such as grapefruit.

CRISPY PEANUT-COATED RICE BALLS

Soft sticky rice balls coated with crunchy peanuts and fried to perfection make a truly tasty snack. Serve with fruity mango chutney mixed with chopped chillies or juicy, sweet sultanas.

INGREDIENTS
(Serves 4)

- 200g/7oz glutinous rice
- salt and white pepper
- 1 onion
- 1 clove garlic
- 300g/10½oz unsalted peanuts
- 2 tbsp groundnut oil
- 2 tbsp chopped fresh parsley or 1 tsp dried
- 1 egg, lightly beaten
- grated rind of 1 lemon
- 2 pinches ground nutmeg
- 2 tbsp cornflour
- 1 litre/1¾ pints vegetable oil, for frying
- 1 red chilli
- 200g/7oz mango chutney
- 1 tbsp sultanas

INGREDIENTS TIP

You can buy glutinous or sticky rice in Asian super-markets. Short grain pudding rice makes a good substitute.

1 Soak the rice for 12 hours. Place in a sieve and rinse with cold water. Put the soaked rice in a saucepan with 500ml/18fl oz of lightly salted water. Simmer over a low heat for 15 minutes until the grains swell and absorb all the water. Remove from the heat and leave to cool.

Step 1

2 Meanwhile, peel and finely chop the onion and garlic. Chop the peanuts and spread out on a plate. Heat the oil in a frying pan and cook the onion and garlic over a low heat for 5 minutes until transparent. Add to the cooked rice and season.

3 Add the parsley to the rice with the egg, lemon rind, nutmeg and cornflour. Mix well, then use your fingers to shape into walnut-sized balls and roll each one in the chopped peanuts. You should have enough mixture to make about 24 balls.

Step 3

4 Heat the vegetable oil in a deep frying pan to 190°C/375°F. Fry the rice balls, 3 or 4 at a time, for 2 minutes until golden. Remove with a slotted spoon and drain on kitchen paper. De-seed and finely chop the chilli. Mix into the mango chutney with the sultanas and serve with the rice balls.

Step 4

Soaking **12** Hours Preparation **45** Min
Cooking **35** Min
Per Serving: 891 kcal/3715 kJ;
24g protein; 59g fat; 70g carbohydrate

TYPICALLY THAI

In Thailand, rice is cooked with fragrant jasmine blossoms so it becomes delicately perfumed with the flowers' aroma. The blossoms are also used to decorate everything from temple altars to restaurant tables and even drinks and cooked dishes.

COOKING TIP

If you have the time, prepare the rice balls 2 or 3 hours ahead of time and chill in the fridge to help firm them up. Just before deep-frying the rice balls, dust your hands with a little flour and re-shape the balls, pressing the mixture together so the balls keep their shape while cooking.

SERVING TIP

Serve a salad of fresh pineapple and mixed lettuce leaves and a chilli dipping sauce with the rice balls.

A tall glass of chilled orange juice and coconut milk in equal quantities is the perfect drink.

GOLDEN THAI RICE WITH PRAWNS

THAILAND

Easy to make and ready in minutes, this Thai speciality combines juicy pink prawns and fresh green spring onions with rice coloured golden by turmeric spice.

INGREDIENTS
(Serves 4)

- 250g/9oz basmati rice
- 1 tsp ground turmeric
- 1 tbsp sesame seeds
- 1 clove garlic
- 1 red chilli
- 2 spring onions
- 3 tbsp groundnut oil
- 1 tbsp lemon juice
- 1 tsp fish sauce
- 250g/9oz small peeled prawns, uncooked
- salt and black pepper

INGREDIENTS TIP
Thai fish sauce, called nam pla, is very salty and is used in many Thai dishes. You can buy it in most supermarkets. Worcestershire or soy sauce can be used instead.

1 Cook the rice in a large saucepan of boiling water with the turmeric for about 10 minutes, or until just tender. Drain in a sieve and rinse with cold water. Spread out the rice on a baking tray to cool and dry.

2 Heat a heavy-based frying pan over a medium heat and add the sesame seeds. Stir for 20–30 seconds until golden. Peel and crush the garlic. Wearing rubber gloves, halve the chilli, remove the seeds and finely chop. Trim, wash and slice the spring onions.

3 Heat the oil in a wok or large frying pan and stir-fry the garlic, chilli and spring onions for 2 minutes, or until lightly cooked.

4 Add the lemon juice and fish sauce to the wok or frying pan and cook, stirring continuously, for 1 minute. Add the prawns and stir-fry for another 3 minutes.

5 Add the cooled rice and stir-fry for about 5 minutes until the rice is thoroughly heated through. Season with salt and pepper.

6 Spoon the fried rice mixture onto a serving plate and sprinkle with the sesame seeds. Serve at once.

Step 1

Step 3

Step 4

Preparation **30** Min Cooking **15** Min
Per Serving: 341 kcal/1434 kJ;
17g protein; 15g fat; 36g carbohydrate

TYPICALLY THAI
The central Thai plateau is one of the most important rice-growing areas of the world. Rice has been cultivated there for over 6000 years, and is a mainstay of Thai cuisine, forming the basis for almost every dish, whether meat, fish or vegetarian.

COOKING TIPS

Immediately after browning the sesame seeds, tip
them out of the pan onto a plate to prevent them
colouring any more • Traditionally, wooden
chopsticks would be used for stirring the food during
cooking, but you will find a spatula or long wooden
spoon works equally well.

SERVING TIP

Serve as a main course, or as an
accompaniment to grilled chicken. Garnish
with chilli flowers (see page 28, step 1).

 A cold light beer makes a refreshing drink to
accompany this spicy dish.

SERVING TIP For a complementary side dish serve a tomato and onion salad.

Try a glass of lassi, a yoghurt drink diluted with iced water and flavoured with sugar or salt.

34

*I*NDIAN LAMB PILAFF

INDIA

INGREDIENTS
(Serves 4)

- 250g/9oz basmati or long grain rice
- 6 tomatoes
- 500g/1lb 2oz lamb, shoulder or leg joint
- 3 onions
- 3 tbsp ghee or vegetable oil
- salt and black pepper
- ½ tsp ground coriander
- ½ tsp ground cumin
- 500ml/18fl oz lamb stock
- 5 whole cloves
- 4 cardamom pods
- 2 cinnamon sticks
- 60g/2½oz flaked almonds
- 4 tbsp sultanas
- 2 tbsp natural yoghurt

INGREDIENTS TIP
Remember to remove the whole spices before serving this dish. If you can't get hold of any lamb stock, then substitute with vegetable stock instead.

The spices flavouring this festive Indian dish are mild rather than hot. Cloves, cardamom, cumin and coriander spice up the rice and the lean, tender lamb, which melts in the mouth.

1 Rinse the rice in a sieve with cold water. Place in a bowl, cover with cold water and leave to soak for 45 minutes. Drain. Pour boiling water over the tomatoes in a bowl, leave for 1 minute, then drain and peel. De-seed and slice.

2 Preheat the oven to 170°C/325°F/Gas 3. Cube the lamb, peel and chop the onions. Heat 1 tablespoon of ghee or oil in a pan over a high heat and fry the meat and half the onion for 3 minutes, stirring constantly, until the meat is sealed. Season, then add coriander, cumin and tomatoes. Remove from the heat and let stand for 10 minutes.

3 Heat 1½ tablespoons of ghee or oil in a flameproof casserole and fry the rest of the onion for 2 minutes. Add the rice and stir for 1 minute over a high heat. Add stock, seasoning, cloves, cardamom, cinnamon and lamb. Cover and bake in the oven for 45 minutes until the rice has absorbed the liquid and the lamb is tender.

4 Heat the remaining ghee or oil in a frying pan and fry the almonds and sultanas for 1 minute. Sprinkle over the pilaff and spoon on the natural yoghurt to garnish.

Step 1

Step 2

Step 4

Soaking **45** Min Preparation **30** Min
Cooking **45** Min
Per Serving: 809 kcal/3381 kJ;
26g protein; 52g fat; 63g carbohydrate

TYPICALLY NORTH INDIAN
The rice in pilaff is always browned first in oil or butter before adding the stock. It's traditionally eaten in northern India during the Holi festival when Indians paint their face with vegetable dyes to greet the arrival of spring and dance through the streets.

CHICKEN BIRYANI

INDIA

Basmati rice and chicken chunks are seasoned with a rich blend of spices — this exotic dish dates from the 16th Century when the great Mogul emperors ruled northern India.

INGREDIENTS
(Serves 4)

- 250g/9oz basmati rice
- 3 cloves garlic
- 4cm/1½in piece root ginger
- ½ tsp ground coriander
- ½ tsp ground cumin
- ¼ tsp cayenne pepper
- 3 tbsp lemon juice
- 150g/5oz natural yoghurt
- 3 onions
- 500g/1lb 2oz chicken breasts, boned
- 50g/2oz ghee or vegetable oil
- salt and black pepper
- 6 strands of saffron
- 4 cardamom pods
- 1 stick cinnamon
- 2 bay leaves
- 100g/4oz cashew nuts

INGREDIENTS TIP
Ghee, or clarified butter, is ideal for frying as it can be heated to a high temperature without burning.

1 Rinse the rice in a sieve with cold water. Transfer to a bowl, cover with cold water and soak for 45 minutes. Peel the garlic and ginger. Chop the garlic and grate the ginger. Mix together with the coriander, cumin, cayenne pepper, lemon juice and yoghurt. Peel and slice the onions. Chop the chicken into bite-sized pieces.

Step 1

2 Heat the ghee or oil in a frying pan over a medium heat and stir-fry the chicken for 3 minutes. Add the onions. Stir-fry for 5 more minutes. Season and remove from the heat.

Step 2

3 Add the chicken and onion to the yoghurt mixture and leave for 30 minutes. Meanwhile, drain the rice and simmer in boiling water for 10 minutes until tender. Preheat the oven to 200°C/400°F/Gas 6.

4 Soak the saffron for 1 minute in 2 tablespoons of hot water. Discard the strands and add the water to the rice with the cardamom pods, cinnamon and bay leaves. Layer the rice and chicken mixture in a greased ovenproof dish. Add 100ml/3½fl oz water, cover and bake for 30 minutes. Dry-fry the cashews in a frying pan and sprinkle over the dish before serving.

Step 4

Soaking **45** Min Preparation **1** Hour
Cooking **30** Min
Per Serving: 675 kcal/2831 kJ;
39g protein; 32g fat; 63g carbohydrate

TYPICALLY INDIAN
Basmati rice is a slender long-grain brown or white rice, grown in the foothills of the Himalayas. Its name, translated from Hindi, means fragrant. The characteristic aroma of basmati rice comes from the mineral-rich melted snow that irrigates the paddy fields where the rice is grown.

COOKING TIP

This is an easy meal to prepare in advance. Cook the rice and chicken mixture separately, allow to cool, then store in covered containers in the fridge. When ready to serve, layer them in the greased ovenproof dish and bake in the oven for 45 minutes, stirring once or twice, to ensure the dish is hot all the way through.

SERVING TIP

Garnish with bay leaves and serve with raita — chopped cucumber mixed with yoghurt and mint.

Serve a dry white wine with a spicy flavour, such as Alsace Gewürztraminer.

3 WAYS WITH STUFFED VEGETABLES

Rice is an ideal filling for courgettes, peppers and aubergines and can be mixed with meat, fish or herbs for delicious variations on a theme.

BASIC COOKED RICE

Preparation **10** Min Cooking **20** Min

(SERVES 4)
- 450ml/¾ pint stock
- 150g/5oz risotto or long grain rice
- salt and black pepper
- 1 onion
- 1 tbsp olive oil
- 50g/2oz Parmesan
- 1 tbsp chopped fresh parsley

1 Bring the stock to the boil in a saucepan. Add the rice and cook for 20 minutes until tender. Season with salt and pepper.

2 Peel and chop the onion. Heat the oil and fry the onion until transparent.

3 Grate the cheese and add to the rice with the onion and parsley.

4 Use large peppers or medium courgettes and aubergines for the stuffing. If you prefer your vegetables soft, cook in boiling water first for 1–2 minutes.

CHEESY COURGETTES

Preparation **20** Min Cooking **40** Min

GREECE

- 1 quantity basic cooked rice
- 4 courgettes
- 1 tsp dried oregano
- 2 eggs
- 300ml/½ pint natural yoghurt
- salt and black pepper
- 100g/4oz goats' cheese

5 Wash and halve the courgettes length-ways. Scoop out the flesh with a spoon.

6 Preheat oven to 200°C/400°F/ Gas 6. Chop the courgette flesh and add to the rice with the herbs. Put courgette shells in a greased ovenproof dish and fill with the rice.

7 Beat the eggs, yoghurt and seasoning together. Chop the cheese and add to the yoghurt, then spoon over the courgettes. Bake for 40 minutes until golden.

TUNA PEPPERS

Preparation **20** Min Cooking **50** Min

SPAIN

- 1 quantity basic cooked rice
- 4 large green peppers
- 2 beef tomatoes
- 2 x 200g/7oz cans tuna in brine
- salt and black pepper
- 1 tsp paprika
- 400g/14oz can chopped tomatoes
- 150ml/¼ pint sherry
- 2 tbsp olive oil
- pimiento-stuffed olives, to garnish

5 Preheat the oven to 180°C/350°F/Gas 4. Wash the peppers, slice off the tops and reserve. Peel, de-seed and chop the tomatoes. Drain the tuna; add to the rice with the chopped fresh tomatoes. Season well and add the paprika.

6 Fill the peppers and replace each top. Mix the canned tomatoes, sherry and 100ml/3½fl oz water in an ovenproof dish. Add the peppers; drizzle with oil. Cover and bake for 50 minutes. Garnish and serve.

AUBERGINES WITH LAMB

Preparation **20** Min Cooking **45** Min

TURKEY

- 1 quantity basic cooked rice
- 4 aubergines
- 1 tbsp olive oil
- 200g/7oz minced lamb
- ½ tsp cinnamon
- ½ tsp paprika
- 25g/1oz butter, cut into pieces

5 Halve the aubergines. Scoop out the flesh and chop.

6 Preheat the oven to 170°C/325°F/Gas 3. Heat the oil and fry the lamb and aubergine for 10 minutes. Add the spices and rice. Spoon the rice into the aubergines. Place in a greased ovenproof dish.

7 Add 150ml/¼ pint water and dot the aubergines with the butter. Cover with foil and bake for 45 minutes until golden brown.

39

$\mathscr{S}$ICILIAN PORK BITES

Herby minced pork and peas, wrapped in a creamy layer of risotto rice and coated in crisp crumbs, hide a meltingly soft centre of creamy mozzarella cheese.

INGREDIENTS
(Serves 4)

- 750ml/1¼ pints chicken stock
- 250g/9oz risotto rice
- 8 strands of saffron
- 1 small egg
- 60g/2½oz Parmesan cheese
- salt and black pepper
- 1 onion
- 1 tbsp olive oil
- 100g/4oz minced pork
- 40g/1½oz frozen peas
- 2 tbsp tomato purée
- ½ tsp dried oregano
- 100g/4oz mozzarella cheese
- 60g/2½oz fresh breadcrumbs
- 1 litre/1¾ pints vegetable oil, for frying
- fresh oregano leaves

INGREDIENTS TIP
To make breadcrumbs, grate day-old bread and leave crumbs uncovered until dry.

1 Bring the stock to the boil, add the rice and saffron strands and simmer for 25 minutes, stirring occasionally until the rice has absorbed the liquid. Leave the rice to cool. Beat the egg, grate the Parmesan, then stir into the rice and season.

Step 1

2 Peel and chop the onion. Heat the oil in a saucepan and fry the pork and onion for 2 minutes. Add the peas and fry for a further 2 minutes, then season with salt and pepper. Stir in the tomato purée, dried oregano and 1 tablespoon water. Cook for a further 6 minutes over a low heat, stirring. Cut the mozzarella into 16 equal squares.

3 Spread the breadcrumbs on a plate. With damp hands, place 1 tablespoon of rice mixture in your palm. Make a hollow in the centre and fill it with 1 tablespoon of pork and a piece of cheese. Cover with another spoonful of rice, roll into a ball and coat in the breadcrumbs. You should make 16 balls.

Step 3

4 Heat the oil in a large frying pan to 190°C/375°F and fry the balls in batches for 3–4 minutes. Drain on kitchen paper and keep warm. Garnish with oregano.

Step 4

Preparation **50** Min Cooking **15** Min
Per Serving: 585 kcal/2450 kJ;
23g protein; 26g fat; 63g carbohydrate

TYPICALLY SICILIAN
The Sicilians call their variations of these rice balls arancini, or little oranges. The name comes from the saffron that the Sicilians added to their mixture to give the balls a golden-orange hue. Sweet oranges grow in Sicily around the volcano Mount Etna.

COOKING TIP

As the pork bites need to be fried in several batches, keep the cooked ones warm in the oven (110°C/225°F/Gas ¼) while you fry the rest. Lift them from the pan with a slotted metal spoon and place on a plate lined with kitchen paper. Do not cover the rice balls or the breadcrumb coating will go soggy.

SERVING TIP

Tomato sauce with a squeeze of fresh orange juice stirred in makes the perfect dipping sauce for these pork bites.

 A Sicilian dry white wine goes well whether these bites are served as a starter or main dish.

41

SERVING TIP Sprinkle chopped fresh herbs, such as parsley or marjoram, over the dish before serving.

 A full-bodied red wine, such as a Rioja, makes a robust accompaniment to paella.

VALENCIAN PAELLA

SPAIN

Many versions of Spain's best-known rice dish exist, but the most famous comes from Valencia where golden saffron rice is mixed with tender chicken, plump prawns and colourful vegetables.

INGREDIENTS
(Serves 4)

- 2 red peppers
- 600g/1lb 5oz beef tomatoes
- 1 large onion
- 3 cloves garlic
- 500g/1lb 2oz skinless, boneless chicken breasts
- 4 tbsp olive oil
- salt and black pepper
- 250g/9oz raw peeled prawns
- 300g/10½oz frozen peas
- 6 strands of saffron
- 1 litre/1¾ pints chicken stock
- 1 tsp paprika
- 400g/14oz risotto rice
- 1 lemon

INGREDIENTS TIP
Cooked prawns could replace the raw ones — stir them in right at the end of cooking to heat through.

1 Preheat the oven to 180°C/350°F/Gas 4. Halve, de-seed and chop the peppers. Peel the tomatoes, de-seed and cut into small pieces. Peel and chop the onion and garlic.

2 Cut the chicken into bite-sized pieces. Heat 2 tablespoons of oil in a paella pan or large frying pan and fry the chicken over a medium heat for 5 minutes. Season and remove. Heat another tablespoon of oil in the pan and fry the prawns for 2 minutes. Remove from the pan.

Step 2

3 Heat the remaining oil in the pan and fry the onion and garlic until transparent. Add the peppers, tomatoes and peas and simmer for 5 minutes. Soak the saffron in 2 tablespoons of stock for 1 minute and stir in with the paprika, salt and pepper.

Step 4

4 Stir the rice into the vegetables, add the remaining stock and simmer for 20 minutes. Add the chicken and prawns.

5 Spoon the paella into an ovenproof dish, cover with foil and bake for 25 minutes until the chicken is cooked. Wash the lemon and cut into 8 wedges. Serve immediately, garnished with the wedges of lemon.

Step 5

Preparation **35** Min Cooking **25** Min
Per Serving: 800 kcal/3375 kJ;
54g protein; 24g fat; 97g carbohydrate

TYPICALLY SPANISH
Valencia, situated on Spain's east coast, is famous for its shellfish. Crabs, mussels and prawns are just some of the ingredients added to Valencian paella. This was traditionally cooked by men in the open air, in large two-handled shallow pans.

ANDALUSIAN CHICKEN

SPAIN

The rice simmers in an aromatic tomato sauce while the chicken is braised gently in paprika and sherry. Rice and meat are then both baked in the oven for a real taste of Spain.

INGREDIENTS
(Serves 4)

- 1.5kg/3½lb chicken joints
- salt and black pepper
- 6 tbsp olive oil
- ¼ tsp ground paprika
- 125ml/4fl oz dry sherry
- 1 bay leaf
- 2 cloves
- 2 large onions
- 3 cloves garlic
- 300g/10½oz long grain rice
- 250ml/9fl oz chicken stock
- 500ml/18fl oz tomato juice
- 1 red pepper
- 1 yellow pepper

INGREDIENTS TIP

The sherry can be replaced with orange juice or extra chicken stock if you prefer the dish without alcohol.

1 Season the chicken with salt and pepper. Heat 3 tablespoons of oil in a frying pan and fry the chicken over a medium heat until golden, about 5 minutes. Add the paprika, sherry, bay leaf and cloves. Cover with a lid and gently simmer for 15 minutes.

Step 1

2 Meanwhile, preheat the oven to 230°C/450°F/Gas 8. Peel and finely chop the onions and garlic. Heat 1 tablespoon of oil in a shallow flameproof dish and gently fry the onions and garlic for 5 minutes until transparent. Add the rice and continue to fry for a further 1 minute.

3 Add the stock and tomato juice, and season with salt and pepper. Simmer for 15 minutes, stirring occasionally.

Step 3

4 Add the chicken and its juices to the rice. Brush 1 tablespoon of oil over the chicken. Bake, uncovered, for 15 minutes until the chicken is tender.

5 Meanwhile, halve, de-seed and slice the peppers. Heat the remaining oil in a frying pan and gently fry the peppers for 5 minutes until tender. Arrange on top of the chicken and serve immediately.

Step 4

Preparation **30** Min Cooking **15** Min
Per Serving: 859 kcal/3613 kJ;
77g protein; 32g fat; 62g carbohydrate

TYPICALLY ANDALUSIAN
The city of Seville in southern Spain reflects its three centuries of Moorish rule in buildings such as the Alcazar palace. It was the Moors who brought rice with them from north Africa — the Spanish word for rice, arroz, comes from the Arabic word ruzz.

COOKING TIPS

If you prefer a more spicy dish, season the chicken with hot, rather than mild, paprika. Both are available from supermarkets • If you do not have a flameproof dish, precook the rice in a saucepan. Cook the other ingredients in a frying pan, then transfer them all to a greased roasting tin before baking.

SERVING TIP

Serve with green olives stuffed with pimiento and almonds, or black olives steeped in olive oil and herbs.

🍷 Try a fruity Spanish rosé, such as Valdepeñas, to accompany this spicy dish.

PROVENCAL RICE AND SPINACH BAKE

SOUTHERN FRANCE

This dish of rice baked with spinach, ham and eggs and topped with a golden cheese crust, is accompanied by an aromatic Provençal sauce of tomatoes, garlic and herbs.

INGREDIENTS
(Serves 4)

- 250g/9oz long grain rice
- salt and black pepper
- 4 shallots
- 200g/7oz cooked ham
- 300g/10½oz spinach leaves
- 1 tbsp olive oil
- 2 eggs
- 2 tbsp chopped fresh parsley or 1 tsp dried
- ½ tsp dried thyme
- ¼ tsp grated nutmeg
- 150g/5oz Emmental cheese

FOR THE SAUCE

- 4 beef tomatoes
- 3 cloves garlic
- 4 tbsp olive oil
- salt and black pepper
- ½ tsp dried mixed herbs
- 50g/2oz pine nuts

INGREDIENTS TIP
Beef tomatoes are extra large with a firm texture. Choose ripe ones for the best flavour.

1 Cook the rice in a saucepan of lightly salted boiling water according to the packet instructions. Drain and leave to cool. Peel and chop the shallots. Slice the ham.

2 Wash the spinach, remove the stalks and drain. Cook the spinach with just the water clinging to the leaves in a large pan, for about 1 minute until it wilts, then drain. Preheat the oven to 180°C/350°F/Gas 4.

3 Heat the oil and fry the shallots for 5 minutes until transparent. Beat the eggs. Mix the ham, parsley, shallots, spinach and eggs into the rice. Season with salt and pepper, and add the thyme and nutmeg.

4 Spoon the rice mixture into a greased ovenproof dish and sprinkle over the Emmental. Bake for 25 minutes until the top is golden brown and firm to the touch.

5 For the sauce, skin the tomatoes and cut into wedges. Peel and chop the garlic. Heat the oil and cook the tomatoes and garlic gently for 15 minutes until pulpy. Season, then add the mixed herbs. Dry-fry the pine nuts. Serve the bake with the tomato sauce, sprinkled with the pine nuts.

Step 3

Step 4

Step 5

Preparation **40** Min Cooking **25** Min
Per Serving: 733 kcal/3057 kJ;
30g protein; 48g fat; 47g carbohydrate

TYPICALLY CAMARGUE
Flamingos and wild horses — not only is the wildlife magical but fruit, vegetables and wine make the Camargue of southern France a land of plenty. A rice called Camargue red rice, grows in the marshlands of the Rhône delta and is used in local dishes.

COOKING TIPS

Spinach needs very little cooking as it wilts quickly
and easily loses its texture. The leaves need rinsing to
remove dirt. Simply leave the water that clings to the
leaves to create enough steam in the pan to cook the
spinach • Alternatively, use ready-to-cook spinach
from supermarkets and microwave it in the bag.

SERVING TIP

A vivid radicchio and tomato salad
with slices of red or green pepper
makes an excellent side dish.

This dish could be served with a chilled rosé
from Provence or a red wine, such as Beaujolais.

VENETIAN RISOTTO

NORTHERN ITALY

INGREDIENTS
(Serves 4)

- 300g/10½oz peas, in the pod
- 1 onion
- 50g/2oz butter
- 250g/9oz risotto rice
- 250ml/9fl oz dry white wine
- 600ml/1 pint hot chicken stock
- 1 clove garlic
- 300g/10½oz cooked, peeled king prawns
- salt and black pepper
- 50g/2oz grated Parmesan cheese

INGREDIENTS TIP

It's important to use a proper risotto rice in this dish, such as Arborio or Carnaroli, as it will become creamy when cooked but still firm to the bite. No other rice will do.

Fresh green peas and king prawns brighten up this classic North Italian dish. The grated Parmesan cheese melts into the rice, making it soft, mellow and creamy.

1 Shell the peas. Peel and chop the onion. Heat 25g/1oz of butter in a large frying pan and gently fry the onion for 5 minutes until transparent.

2 Add the peas and rice to the frying pan and stir until coated with the butter. Pour in the white wine and bring to the boil, stirring constantly. Continue to cook, stirring, until all of the liquid has evaporated.

3 Stir in the hot stock. Lower the heat and simmer gently, uncovered, for about 30 minutes or until the rice is tender and has absorbed the stock.

4 Meanwhile, peel and finely chop the garlic. Heat 15g/½oz of butter in another frying pan and fry the prawns and garlic over a medium heat for about 4 minutes, stirring constantly. Season well.

5 Taste to check the rice and peas are done. If the rice is chewy, or the peas are hard, continue to simmer, adding a little more hot stock or water. Stir in the remaining butter and the grated Parmesan cheese. Add the prawns and garlic and fluff up the rice before serving.

Step 1

Step 4

Step 5

Preparation **30** Min Cooking **30** Min
Per Serving: 551 kcal/2316 kJ;
32g protein; 17g fat; 63g carbohydrate

TYPICALLY VENETIAN

Risi e bisi, or rice and peas, is the most aristocratic of all Italy's risottos. It used to be served every year on St Mark's Day, 25 April, at an important banquet held in Venice and was made with the first young peas from the gardens around the lagoon.

COOKING TIP
Make sure the chicken stock is hot when you add it to the rice, so the temperature in the pan does not drop and the rice continues cooking. Peel the shells from the prawns and remove the black vein before adding them to the pan but leave the tail on for a decorative effect.

SERVING TIP
Serve with lemon wedges — their juice will heighten the delicate flavour of the seafood.

 A dry, white Orvieto is ideal with this dish. Chill it for several hours before serving.

CLASSIC MILANESE RISOTTO

NORTHERN ITALY

Risotto rice, cooked slowly with white wine, saffron and cheese, absorbs all their tantalizing flavours. The secret of success when making this dish couldn't be simpler — just keep stirring!

INGREDIENTS
(Serves 4)

- 1 large onion
- 50g/2oz butter
- 400g/14oz risotto rice
- 100ml/3½fl oz white wine
- 1.2 litres/2 pints hot chicken stock
- salt and white pepper
- ½ tsp saffron threads
- 60g/2½oz Parmesan cheese
- fresh basil, to garnish

INGREDIENTS TIP

Saffron, the dried stigmas of the purple-flowering crocus, is the world's most expensive spice. It takes over 14,000 saffron threads to make just 1 ounce. It has a slightly bitter taste and is a strong dye. Only a few threads are needed to flavour and colour a dish.

1 Peel and chop the onion. Heat 25g/1oz of butter in a large frying pan and fry the onion for 5 minutes until transparent.

2 Add the rice and stir until each grain is evenly coated with butter. Add the white wine and continue stirring until it has been absorbed by the rice.

Step 2

3 Gradually add most of the stock to the pan, a ladleful at a time, stirring frequently and adding more stock as the rice absorbs it. After about 30–40 minutes the rice should be tender and will have absorbed most of the stock. Season with salt and pepper.

Step 3

4 Place the saffron strands in 1 tablespoon hot stock and add to the rice. Test the rice — if it is not yet soft, continue to simmer, adding more stock as necessary.

5 The risotto is ready when the rice has a soft creamy consistency, but the individual grains are still a little chewy in the centre. Stir in the remaining butter, and season. Grate the Parmesan and stir in. Garnish with fresh basil. Serve immediately.

Step 4

Preparation **15** Min Cooking **45** Min
Per Serving: 551 kcal/2325 kJ;
13g protein; 18g fat; 86g carbohydrate

TYPICALLY MILANESE

A special short grain rice called arborio is used by the Italians for making their world-famous saffron risotto. The recipe originated in the elegant city of Milan, and the arborio rice grows in the valley of the Po River, an area just south of Milan.

COOKING TIP

Saffron threads need soaking in a little hot water or stock to release their colour before they are added to a dish. When the dish is cooked, the threads can be left in or removed. Powdered saffron is also available and can be substituted. Use half a teaspoon and add directly to the dish.

SERVING TIP

Fresh sage leaves, lightly fried in butter, make a colourful and aromatic garnish for a risotto.

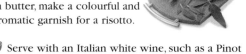

Serve with an Italian white wine, such as a Pinot Grigio from the Friuli region north of Venice.

NORMANDY CHEESE AND RICE SOUFFLE

NORTHERN FRANCE

A tasty combination of rice, chives and Emmental make up this sophisticated French soufflé. Bake until golden brown and serve with an authentic creamy, cider sauce.

INGREDIENTS
(Serves 4)

- 200g/7oz risotto rice
- 750ml/1¼ pints chicken stock
- 40g/1½oz butter, plus extra for greasing
- 40g/1½oz plain flour
- 250ml/9fl oz milk
- salt and white pepper
- ¼ tsp grated nutmeg
- 4 eggs
- 150g/5oz grated Emmental cheese
- 2 tbsp chopped fresh chives or 1 tsp dried

FOR THE SAUCE
- 125ml/4fl oz dry cider
- 250ml/9fl oz double cream
- 15g/½oz butter
- salt and white pepper
- squeeze of lemon juice
- 2 tbsp chopped parsley or 2 tsp dried

1 Cook the rice in the stock for 20 minutes, or until the rice is tender and has absorbed the stock. Leave to cool. Melt the butter in a saucepan over a low heat, stir in the flour and cook for 1 minute. Take off the heat and stir in the milk, then bring to the boil, stirring, until the sauce thickens. Season with salt and pepper and add the nutmeg.

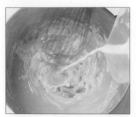

Step 1

2 Separate the eggs. Mix the yolks into the sauce, then stir in the rice. Whisk the egg whites until stiff, then fold them into the rice with the cheese and chives.

3 Preheat the oven to 150°C/300°F/Gas 2. Grease a 1.5 litre/2½ pint soufflé dish. Spoon in the mixture and bake for 35 minutes, or until puffed, golden brown and firm to the touch.

Step 2

4 While the soufflé is cooking, make the sauce. Heat the cider in a saucepan and simmer until reduced by half. Add the cream and boil to reduce by half again. Lower the heat and stir in the butter. Season with salt and pepper. Add the lemon juice and parsley, then pour the sauce into a jug. Serve the soufflé as soon as it is cooked, with the sauce.

Step 3

Preparation **40** Min Cooking **35** Min
Per Serving: 838 kcal/3491 kJ;
22g protein; 61g fat; 52g carbohydrate

TYPICALLY NORMANDY

Butter, cream and apples are the best known products from Normandy. All are used in local dishes, such as Poulet Vallée d'Auge (chicken with cream, apples and brandy). The prolific apple crop is used to produce cider, wine and the famous liqueur called Calvados.

COOKING TIPS

The soufflé can be baked in individual (200ml/7fl oz) soufflé dishes and served as a starter. The cooking time will be about 10 minutes less • Instead of the cider cream sauce, you could serve a ready-made tomato pasta sauce with the soufflé. Just heat through in a saucepan, then pour into a serving jug.

SERVING TIP

Serve a mixed tomato and lettuce salad, tossed with a dressing of olive oil, wine vinegar and fresh herbs.

A glass of apple or pineapple juice would make a refreshing accompaniment to the soufflé.

SERVING TIP A tomato and cucumber salad, served on a bed of lettuce, goes well with this dish.

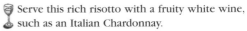 Serve this rich risotto with a fruity white wine, such as an Italian Chardonnay.

ALPINE MUSHROOM AND HERB RISOTTO

SWITZERLAND

This risotto owes its intense aroma and flavour to the dried mushrooms and fresh herbs used to flavour it. Saffron adds its characteristic golden hue to the pearly grains of rice.

INGREDIENTS

(Serves 4)

- 40g/1½oz dried mushrooms
- 1 large onion
- 50g/2oz butter
- 1 litre/1¾ pints chicken stock
- 400g/14oz risotto rice
- 250ml/9fl oz dry white wine
- 50g/2oz Parmesan cheese
- 5 fresh borage or sage leaves
- ½ tsp saffron powder
- salt and white pepper

INGREDIENTS TIP

Dried cep mushrooms are available in packets from larger supermarkets and delicatessens. Although fairly expensive, you only need a few mushrooms to transform a simple dish into a rich and full-flavoured feast.

1 In a small bowl, soak the dried mushrooms in 200ml/7fl oz warm water for at least 30 minutes until doubled in size. Peel and finely chop the onion.

2 Drain the mushrooms in a sieve and press out the remaining water into a small bowl, reserving the liquid. Slice or chop any large mushrooms. Heat 15g/½oz of butter in a large frying pan, add the onion and fry over a medium heat for 5 minutes until golden brown. Add the mushrooms and fry for 1 minute.

3 Heat the stock in a saucepan. Add the rice to the mushrooms and stir well. Stirring frequently, add the wine and stock, 150ml/¼ pint at a time. Make sure the liquid is absorbed by the rice before adding more. The rice should have absorbed all the stock and be cooked after about 30 minutes.

4 Grate the Parmesan cheese. Wash and dry the borage or sage and chop finely. Stir into the rice with the saffron. Add the remaining butter and the reserved water from the mushrooms. Season, sprinkle with cheese and serve.

Step 2

Step 3

Step 4

Soaking **30** Min Preparation **10** Min
Cooking **30** Min

Per Serving: 572 kcal/2411 kJ;
13g protein; 18g fat; 86g carbohydrate

TYPICALLY SWISS

Tessin is the sunniest and most southern part of Switzerland. Both its language and cuisine have a strong Italian influence. Risottos are especially popular in the region's isolated villages and this dish is typically made with the locally produced hard cheese, Sbrinz.

RICE RING WITH CREAMY RAGOUT

GERMANY

Baked rice rings are very popular in Germany. Here, tender spring vegetables and juicy prawns in a creamy sauce are attractively arranged in a fluffy rice crown.

INGREDIENTS
(Serves 6)

- butter for greasing
- 350g/12oz long grain rice
- 1litre/1¾ pints hot chicken stock
- 175ml/6fl oz double cream
- 2 small egg yolks
- 100g/4oz grated Parmesan cheese

FOR THE RAGOUT

- 200g/7oz green beans
- 200g/7oz baby carrots
- 250g/9oz asparagus tips
- 75g/3oz frozen peas
- 25g/1oz butter
- 1 tbsp plain flour
- 250ml/9fl oz whipping cream
- 150ml/¼ pint chicken stock
- salt and black pepper
- pinch of ground nutmeg
- pinch of ground paprika
- 225g/8oz peeled prawns
- flat-leaved parsley, to garnish

1 Preheat the oven to 200°C/400°F/Gas 6. Butter a 24cm/9½in ring mould. Cook the rice in the stock for 20 minutes, or until tender. Stir in the cream, egg yolks and cheese until well combined. Spoon into the ring mould, pressing down firmly. Chill until ready to bake (see Cooking tip).

Step 1

2 Wash, trim and halve the green beans and the carrots. Remove any woody ends from the asparagus and cut into bite-sized pieces. Bake the rice ring for 20–25 minutes, or until golden.

3 Meanwhile, bring a pan of water to the boil. Add the carrots, then cover and simmer for 5 minutes. Add the beans, asparagus and peas. Cover and simmer for a further 5 minutes, or until tender.

Step 4

4 Melt the butter in a saucepan. Add the flour and cook, stirring, for 2 minutes. Off the heat, whisk in the cream and stock. Return to the heat and stir until thickened. Season, then add the nutmeg and paprika. Add the prawns and simmer gently until heated through. Turn the rice ring out onto a plate and spoon the ragoût into the middle. Garnish with parsley and serve.

Step 4

Preparation **40** Min Cooking **20** Min
Per Serving: 756 kcal/3155 kJ;
26g protein; 46g fat; 65g carbohydrate

TYPICALLY SAXON

Before the First World War, Saxony was a separate duchy in eastern Germany. Creamy ragoûts were a popular first course on festive occasions in Saxony. Traditionally, this dish would have been made to welcome back Spring and look forward to the new harvest.

COOKING TIP

The rice for the ring can be prepared in advance. Follow Step 1, then cover the ring and keep in the fridge for up to 1 day. Allow the mould to return to room temperature before baking or the cooking time will be affected. Cook and turn out the ring only when you are ready to serve it.

SERVING TIP

Garnish with small crescents of puff pastry, baked until golden, to add a slight crunch.

A dry Riesling from the Rhine Valley goes well with this rice dish.

WINTER RICE AND PORK CASSEROLE

BULGARIA

Rice, potatoes and meat simmer away in a tasty chicken stock to make this warming casserole. Green peppers and tomato add a splash of colour and a sweet, mellow flavour.

INGREDIENTS

(Serves 4)

- 1 large onion
- 1 clove garlic
- 4 green peppers
- 400g/14oz Charlotte or other waxy potatoes
- 1 beef tomato
- 500g/1lb 2oz pork shoulder
- 3 tbsp sunflower oil
- salt and black pepper
- 2 tbsp chopped fresh parsley or 1 tsp dried
- 150g/5oz long grain rice
- 2 tbsp paprika
- 500ml/18fl oz hot chicken stock

INGREDIENTS TIP

Pork shoulder is a good cut for casseroling because it does not dry out and tenderizes beautifully. Trim any fat from the meat before cutting into cubes.

1 Peel and finely chop the onion and garlic. Cut the peppers in half and remove the seeds and stalks. Peel the potatoes and cut into even-sized pieces.

2 Put the tomato into a bowl and cover with boiling water. Leave for 30 seconds then remove and run under cold water. Cut a slit in the skin and peel off. Scoop out the seeds and dice the flesh. Cut the pork into bite-sized pieces, removing any fat.

Step 2

3 Heat 2 tablespoons of oil in a saucepan and brown the pork for 5 minutes, stirring occasionally with a wooden spatula. Season with salt and pepper and remove from the pan.

4 Fry the onion and garlic in the saucepan with the remaining oil for 3 minutes until transparent, stirring occasionally. Add the parsley, peppers, tomato, potatoes and rice. Season with paprika.

Step 3

5 Gradually add the pork to the pan, then slowly stir in the stock. Cover with a lid and simmer gently for about 45 minutes, or until the meat is tender and the potatoes and vegetables are cooked. Serve immediately.

Step 5

Preparation **30** Min Cooking **45** Min
Per Serving: 664 kcal/2771 kJ;
26g protein; 41g fat; 52g carbohydrate

TYPICALLY BULGARIAN

This hearty dish is known as Guivech in its native Bulgaria and it would be made with either pork or lamb depending on the religion of the cook's family. The vegetables can also vary, although peppers would always be used.

COOKING TIP

The best way to brown the pork, and seal in its
juices, is to fry it in small batches. If the meat is added
all at once to the frying pan it will lower the
temperature of the pan and may stew the meat rather
than seal it. Remove the pieces when browned and
put to one side on a plate, until required.

SERVING TIP

In Bulgaria, casseroles are served
with Airjan — a cool, spicy drink
made from frothy yoghurt and herbs.

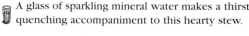

A glass of sparkling mineral water makes a thirst-
quenching accompaniment to this hearty stew.

SERVING TIP Serve with a green salad to complement the rich flavour of the smoked fish.

A lightly chilled white wine or tangy cordial, such as elderflower, makes a refreshing accompaniment.

$\mathcal{K}$EDGEREE

GREAT BRITAIN

INGREDIENTS
(Serves 4)

- 350g/12oz smoked haddock fillet
- 1 bay leaf
- 1 large onion
- 50g/2oz butter
- 200g/7oz long grain rice
- 1 tsp curry powder
- 600ml/1 pint hot fish or vegetable stock
- 2 tsp lemon juice
- 2 hard-boiled eggs
- black pepper

TO GARNISH

- 2 tbsp chopped fresh parsley
- lemon wedges
- sprigs of fresh dill

INGREDIENTS TIP
To give your dish a vivid yellow colour add 1 tsp turmeric instead of curry powder. Use sparingly as turmeric has a strong, slightly bitter flavour.

Lightly curried rice is combined with smoked haddock and hard-boiled eggs for a deliciously creamy dish that can be served as a light supper or best of all for breakfast.

1 Place the haddock in a large pan with the bay leaf and cover with sufficient cold water to cover it. Bring to the boil, lower the heat and cover. Simmer for about 5 minutes until cooked through, when the flesh begins to flake easily with a fork. Drain, remove the skin and bones, and flake the flesh into small pieces with a fork.

2 Peel and slice the onion. Melt 25g/1oz of butter in a saucepan and cook the onion for 5 minutes until transparent. Stir in the rice and curry powder and cook for 2 minutes.

3 Pour in the stock and bring to the boil. Cover the pan, lower the heat and simmer for 10–15 minutes until the rice is tender and has absorbed all the stock.

4 Add the flaked fish, lemon juice, and remaining butter. Peel the hard-boiled eggs and cut into quarters. Stir into the rice mixture and season with pepper.

5 Reheat gently for 2–3 minutes, stirring occasionally so the rice does not stick to the bottom of the pan. Spoon into a warmed serving dish, sprinkle with parsley and add lemon wedges and dill sprigs to garnish.

Step 1

Step 3

Step 4

Preparation **20** Min Cooking **30** Min
Per Serving: 387 kcal/1630 kJ;
22g protein; 15g fat; 44g carbohydrate

TYPICALLY ENGLISH
Kedgeree became a popular dish among the Victorian landed gentry — a hearty breakfast fortifying them for the day's game shooting. The ingredients have changed over the years, but originate from an Indian recipe of spiced onions and lentils called Kitchri.

DICTIONARY OF TERMS

Rice is an excellent foil for almost any ingredient. Its mild taste and texture combine well with vegetables, seafood and meat and flavourings such as spices, herbs and sauces.

Cardamom is an aromatic spice derived from the ginger family. Used mainly in Indian and North African dishes, it is available either ground or as green pods. The pods contain fine black seeds that can be crushed and sprinkled over rice to go with a curry.

Cayenne pepper is a fiery, orange-red spice, named after the part of South America where it originated. It is made from the flesh and seeds of the smallest, hottest chillies and is usually sold ground. Use cayenne pepper sparingly as it is pungent and very hot and will overpower other more delicate flavours.

Chillies are available fresh, either red or green and in many sizes and strengths, ground or as a ready-made sauce. It is difficult to guess the strength of chillies, but often the smallest and narrowest are also the hottest. Ground chilli powder is available in hot and mild flavours, but it is frequently mixed with other spices as well. Chilli powder needs to be fried in a little oil for 1–2 minutes to release its flavour and aroma. It is best suited to dishes such as curries or Chilli con Carne where the powder can

COOKING LONG GRAIN RICE

Allow 50–75g/2–3oz rice per serving. The easiest way to measure rice is to use the cup method. One cup — capacity 225ml/8fl oz — of uncooked rice weighs about 150g/5oz. When cooked, one cup of rice yields 375g/13oz. The following methods are the most common ways of cooking rice:

PAN-COOKED RICE
For 4 servings, heat 1 tbsp oil in a saucepan. Fry 1 chopped onion until transparent. Stir in 350g/12oz rice, cook for 1 minute. Pour in 500ml/18fl oz chicken or vegetable stock. Bring to the boil, cover and cook over a low heat for 20 minutes, stirring, until the rice is tender and has absorbed the stock.

STEAMED RICE
Soak the rice in cold water for 30 minutes, then steam in a sieve over a large saucepan of boiling water for 40 minutes. Alternatively, use a wok with a bamboo steaming basket, lined with a cotton cloth.

PRESSURE-COOKED RICE
You generally use 1 cup of water per cup of rice in the bottom of the pressure cooker. Follow the manufacturer's instructions as to exactly how much water is needed. Cooking usually takes about 7 minutes, but allow longer for brown rice.

BOILED RICE
Rinse the rice and add to a pan of salted boiling water. Cook for 10 minutes, or according to packet instructions, stirring frequently. The rice is cooked as soon as the centre is no longer brittle, but still has bite. Drain, fluff the rice with a fork and serve.

OVEN-COOKED RICE
Preheat the oven to 180°C/350°F/Gas 4. Boil the water and combine it with the rice, salt and butter in a casserole dish. Cover and bake for 25–30 minutes or until the rice is tender.

be fried along with the onions and meat at the start of the recipe. As an

alternative, you can also use chilli sauce, which is a liquid version of the powder, and is available in both hot and mild strengths. Add as little or as much as you want.

Cumin is a spice often used in Indian and North African dishes. It has a mildly hot, sweet flavour and aroma and is sold ground or as seeds. The ground spice should be dry-fried to bring out its flavour, then it can be added to plain boiled rice for a delicious accompaniment to a mild curry or meat stew.

Dried fruits such as raisins, sultanas, apricots and dates often add flavour to Middle Eastern rice pilaffs. Their sweetness contrasts well with the spicy flavours in the accompanying dishes. Dried fruits are also served as side dishes in India and the Middle East to eat on their own or to sprinkle over rice dishes such as Biryani.

Ghee is a clarified butter used extensively in Indian cookery. It is particularly good for frying as it can be heated to very high temperatures without burning.

Groundnut oil is a light, golden oil made from peanuts. It has a nutty aroma and bland flavour that does not overshadow other ingredients. It can be heated to a very high temperature, making it an ideal all-purpose oil.

Peas are often combined with rice in both Italian and Far Eastern dishes. Fresh shelled peas and frozen are suitable. Mange tout and sugarsnap peas are added to Chinese rice stir-fries and the pods are edible too.

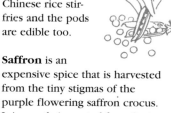

Saffron is an expensive spice that is harvested from the tiny stigmas of the purple flowering saffron crocus. It is mostly imported from Spain and has an aromatic, slightly bitter taste. It can be bought dried and in powder form. To use bottled saffron threads, soak in liquid, then discard the strands and use the liquid.

Sambal oelek is a hot and spicy red chilli based paste from Indonesia and Thailand. It can be added to dishes or served as a dipping sauce or accompaniment to Far Eastern recipes such as Satay. Sambal oelek is available from larger supermarkets and Asian shops. It can also be made at home by puréeing red chillies with a little oil to make a paste.

STORING COOKED RICE

Ideally, rice should be eaten on the day it is cooked as it attracts harmful bacteria. If it is necessary to cook rice ahead, cool it quickly in a sieve under cold running water. Drain the rice well, then transfer it to a freezer bag. Seal and store in the fridge for up to 24 hours. To reheat, either steam the rice in a colander over a pan of boiling water or pierce the bag before placing it in a microwave — allow 5 minutes per 450g/1lb on full power.

Tomato is a popular flavouring for rice dishes. Canned plum tomatoes can be bought whole or chopped, either plain or flavoured with garlic, herbs and spices. Baby cherry tomatoes are available fresh or canned. Tomato purée adds a concentrated tomato flavour to dishes, and a slightly smoky-flavoured alternative is now available made using sun-dried tomatoes. Passata, or sieved tomatoes, is sold as a thick sauce in cartons or jars. Tomato juice is sold in cans or cartons and has a thinner consistency. Red pesto sauce, an Italian paste of sun-dried tomatoes mixed with basil, pine nuts, olive oil and Parmesan cheese, is delicious stirred into rice or pasta dishes.

INDEX

Acknowledgements

Picture Credits
All cover and recipe pictures:
Meister Verlag/International Masters Publisher B.V.
Karl Adamson, Michael Brauner, Dorothee Gödert, Neil Mersh
Peter Rees, Philip Wilkins
Agency pictures: *Introduction:* Di Girolamo, Gottschalk, IFA, Koch,
Superstock, TPL, Transglobe
Pictures for the 'Typically' Sections
Bavaria: Weissing, page 55; Bilder Pur: Janicek, page 58; Robert Harding:
Allgöwer, page 40; Chotas, page 48; Gruß, page 44; Heisch: page 10; IFA:
Diaf, pages 6, 9, 52; Fiedler, page 22; Maier, page 46; Michler, page 30;
Otto, page 56; Image Bank: Chernush, page 36; Curto, page 12; Melford,
page 14; Newman, page 17; Helga Lade: Bav, page 50; Fey, page 32; Look:
Heeb, page 18; Johaentges, page 24; Okapia: Büttner, page 27;
Schapowalow: Thiele, page 43; The Stock Market, pages 35, 61; Stadler,
page 28; Tony Stone: Randkley, page 18; Camille, page 44

Measuring Ingredients
Tsp - teaspoon, Tbsp - tablespoon
Teaspoons and tablespoons are level and measured using standard
measuring spoons.
Follow either metric or imperial measurements and don't mix the two.